I0016624

Roadmap to Software Devel

By Christine Axsmith

Special thanks to my husband Justin, who is always supportive and fun.

Copyright 2018 Christine Axsmith
Published by Success Without College Publications at KDP
Amazon

Table of Contents

Roadmap to Software Developer - $uccess Without College

Page 3

You Can Do It, Too

Three little boys were always late for school. They would wait for the train to come by and run through the smoke it left and then go to school.

One of those boys went to prison for life; the other went to a hospital for the criminally insane, and the third little boy was my Father.

My uncle, a former President of the AFL-CIO for Pennsylvania, called my father the "most successful person he had ever known." I agree.

In $uccess Without College - Roadmap to Software Developer, I am telling you what my Father and others taught me about real success, American-style.

Life is choices. Every day of your life you make a hundred little decisions that either point you towards your goals or not. You can choose to sleep in all day, or not. Or you can decide to take half an hour a day to learn a new language or to play the guitar. It's up to you.

This book is for the people who are willing to choose work and courage over hiding behind conventional wisdom. If you are willing to work as hard as someone who goes to college - on your own, without nagging - then you can be a software developer. My Father could only afford two years of college because I was born. But he worked for hours on weekends, evenings, and holidays to prepare for his professional engineering license test, even though most people who take that test already have a four-year degree.

He failed the test the first time, but kept working at it until he succeeded. My Father is an amazing man in many respects.

My most indelible memories growing up were sitting with my Father and my sisters at the dining room table, all of us doing math and studying for a test. Give the children in your family the gift my Father gave me; a family memory of studying and working together.   Your decision to take this path will affect everyone around you, as well as yourself. Do it! You have only the future in front of you.

Not everyone has the option of college.   This is not an anti-college book. It is a book for any age for people who want to work hard. You just have to want it.   Choose your future, don't let it just happen to you.

The Big Lie

You don't need college to be an American success story. The idea that college is a necessity is new. It never used to be that way.

Since 2008, the United States has lost millions of jobs. Many of those jobs are not coming back. RIght now, many attorneys are being replaced by software programs, where someone can file a lawsuit just by answering a few questions on a website. No one thought that would start happening when factories were sent overseas. They thought it would happen to somebody else.

But there are jobs that cannot be sent overseas, or replaced by a robot. These are the types of jobs my books will describe to you.

I want to help you. My superpower is learning a new career from scratch. I started my professional life writing information systems security policies, have tested large information systems, started a dog walking business, became a court-appointed attorney for the elderly and mentally disabled, started a sole practitioner law firm focused on real estate litigation, and now am a writer.

We are all told that the unemployment rate is very low, but that isn't true. It is actually around 10%. The low unemployment numbers reported on the news are based on phoning 3,500 people during a weekday and asking if they have a job. There is no fact-checking at all. Nobody looks to see if they are telling the truth. Actually, the last thing they want in those numbers is the truth. If people knew the extent of America's unemployment, they would be even angrier than they were during the last election.

There is another number economists use to determine the unemployment rate: U6 unemployment rate. That number is calculated by counting the number of people who were getting a W-2 paycheck and subtracting the number of people who were on W-2 jobs and then later received unemployment benefits and who did not get another job. As of the writing of this book, the unemployment rate, the real one, is 9.4%.

Of course, if you are being told that the unemployment rate is historically low and you don't have a job, it implies that you are at fault. Also not true.

It is equally untrue that you need a college degree to be a success in America. You are being told, and even sold, the idea that college debt is a smart move to get a degree. The underlying promise in this sales pitch is that, with a degree, you will be able to get a well-paying job.

I graduated law school with so much debt; it defined my choices for the next 15 years. I couldn't take jobs I wanted, or own a car because of my student loan debt. If there is some way to help young people avoid this circumstance I want to do it. So I wrote this book.

Nowhere in the famous Horatio Alger stories based on The American Dream does anybody go to college. Many successful Americans did not go to college at first. That can be you. This book is for people who want to become software developers. Other books in this series $uccess Without College Roadmap will be written for other types of work. Each book will be a standalone roadmap to a profession, not just a job.

A profession means you have valuable skills that you can take with you for the rest of your career. A career is how you build those skills from one job to another. A successful career is when people in your industry know your name, know some of your work history, and can take a good guess at your skill set - just by hearing your name. A profession is the most important investment you will make in your lifetime. Your skills are something that can never be taken from you. If your profession is going to be software development, then you need to invest time and effort to get there.

Nothing in life is about passing a test and getting what you want. A certificate does not make you a software developer, and it won't get you a job. That's why getting a college degree is not a recipe for success.

This book explains the real, old-fashioned American Dream. It is different from the you-must-go-to-college-or-your-life-is-over message. Success is not what you thought it was. Neither is what success looks like, let alone how to get there. This book tells you how to see success, and how to go and get it.

Your Advantage in Not Having a Degree

No Student Loans

These days, many college graduates have huge debts and no serious prospect of work. The "deal" had been broken where a job could be expected if you graduated from college. Now high school students are encouraged to take out student loans, and no one pretends that they should expect a job upon graduation from college.

However, did anyone tell you how to become a programmer without college? That's what this book is about. Also, you will help yourself a great deal if you have a programming buddy to learn with. This has been proven to make learning software development easier and faster.

You can take control of your life, and your career, by systematically following this Roadmap to $uccess, and then going and getting it. It takes social courage to be good at something. You put doing a task first. You work hard, even with doubts. You don't let what other people say or do take you off the track to your goal. That is success.

Why Should You Be Hired Over a College Graduate?

- You work harder.
- You are mature and have had jobs with responsibility in the past, and your resume reflects this.
- Good school attendance record.
- You will show up on time and get the task completed.
- You don't need to be told how important you are, or what a good job you are doing more than once in six months.
- You know that your opinion doesn't mean much, and what you can do means much more.

Roadmap to Software Developer provides the step-by-step plan to becoming a software developer. Many large companies like Microsoft and Google will require a degree. But most programming jobs are not at places like that. They are in manufacturing companies, car sale companies, grocery, and retail companies. That's your in.

And you won't need a degree.

Who This Book is For

Roadmap to Software Developer is written for anyone who wants have a starting point and a roadmap to becoming a software developer without getting a computer science degree. This book is to enable anyone who can do the work to get this career.

Roadmap to Software Developer is designed to help someone become a computer programmer, no matter the level of experience with computer programming. It provides a roadmap to follow in an overwhelming sea of information on this topic. It provides many links to free self-education.

What This Book Will Do

Roadmap to Software Developer gives you everything you need to get started on a software development career without college. Besides, a college class is a horrible way to learn to write software. The projects are boring and useless. There is no interaction with the users of your application, either.

You need a good starting point for your own self-education. $uccess Without College - Roadmap to Software Developer will tell you about teaching yourself software development, and how to get a job from there.

"College" is a word that is shorthand for a lot of things other than education. When employers ask for a "college degree," they really want some professionalism, middle-class appearance and manners, maturity, and moderate intelligence, and discipline. You don't need to get into $100,000 of debt to offer this to an employer.

$uccess Without College - Roadmap to Software Developer will tell you what those middle-aged hiring managers are secretly thinking - and worrying about - when they interview you. I know, because I was one of them.

What This Book Won't Do

Roadmap to Software Developer will empower you, but there are things it cannot do for you.

If you are going to buck the trend of the people and community around you, you need to be prepared for certain things. You are going to start to feel disconnected from that community. You are going to feel scared. Norman Podhoretz wrote an excellent book "Making It" about what it feels like to rise to the middle class. It is an old book, and probably won't be in your local library. He describes his feelings of awkwardness around the new people he met. He shows his shame at not understanding what they are talking about. And this was one brilliant guy. Yes, his story does include going to college, but his emotional journey is one that you may have to make as well.

When I started school in Philadelphia, it was a dramatic change from the small town I had known all my life. Market Street divided the campus and was a major, busy street. The problem was, I had no experience crossing a busy four lane street in a major city and would often get stuck in the middle, on the double lines, when the light changed, while traffic buzzed right by me. I was too scared to move. People had to run out to the middle of Market Street, people I didn't even know, and walk me to the curb.

This happened repeatedly. Other students knew me as the girl who would get stuck in the middle of the street for years. It was very humiliating, plus I was the only one this happened to. Seriously. I can look back on that feeling of shame and say, "So what?" That's right. Who cares? Would I trade a lifetime of opportunity and growth to avoid feeling that again? No. Don't you, either. What embarrasses you right now will make a great story at a party in later years. Trust me. What makes an interesting dinner guest is someone who laughs at their mistakes, not someone who tells everyone about their accomplishments. Let other people do that for you.

You can't just say, "I am getting a professional job and everything else about the way I act and talk are staying the same." Being a professional also means being middle class in appearance and manners. That choice will influence your private life, too. One book to read, although it is from 1980, is "Class" by Paul Fossell. He was kind of nasty guy, so don't get too depressed. But his insights on college as a middle class stamp are on target.

Most people cannot do it. They are not strong enough. They are too afraid of the envy and resentment of family and friends. Now, most likely, family and friends will be very proud of you. But the fear that there will be a separation is enough for most young people to quit their dreams. That's a choice affecting the rest of your life.

Another important thing this book will not do for you is give you maturity and discipline. If you need to be reminded five times to get a chore or homework done, you will not succeed in anything, let alone being a software developer, until that changes. If you want to educate yourself, you need to work many hours to do it. You will need to review what you have done and look for ways to improve it. You will need to listen to the users of the application you created rather than arguing with them and calling them stupid. If you don't understand a term in this book or a website, you will need to look it up until you do understand it.

The words used in software development are always changing, and writing a book to give them to you will mean the book will never get finished. Besides, that is not the purpose of this book. $uccess Without College - Roadmap to Software Developer gives the starting point for your own self-education. No one is trying to make this easy for you. If you want this path, you will need to work for it as much as anyone going to college has to work to get their degree.

Wake up and see what is going on out there. This is difficult because you are being told that you need to go to college; college is the only way to be an American success, and only losers don't go to college. The news supports this view and TV shows endorse this view. It is the lie that you will make enough money if you just get that college degree.

Not true.

The American Dream vs. The American Day Dream

The American Dream Defined:

"*That dream of a land in which life should be better and richer and fuller for everyone, with opportunity for each according to ability or achievement.*"
- James Treslow Adams.

Notice it doesn't say anything about college or student loans.

What you have been told is a lie. You can spend a lot of money and time investing in this lie, or you can choose something different for yourself.

Owning a small business that is successful, where the owner can earn the respect of his peers and community, and gather a small bit of wealth about themselves and their family is the American Dream. It is where hard work and honesty lead to material comfort and respect. There is no need to lie and steal to survive, which is the reality in other places.

A "dream" does not mean something is not true; it just means that it is a story we tell ourselves about ourselves. It reveals the core values of a society and a country. The "American Dream" is one of the most powerful on Earth.

The American Dream is that anyone can rise above his or her circumstances to achieve success in the United States. If you are willing to work hard, be honest, take risks and not get into debt, the American Dream promises you success in America.

The American Day Dream is what advertising sells you. It is the lives shown in movies where a waitress can afford to live in a large apartment in Manhattan, or where an Assistant District Attorney drives a Mercedes. It is where everyone has a large, flat screen TV.

The American Dream is not getting into debt.

The American Day Dream causes you to look at your neighbors to judge yourself. It creates fears of teeth that aren't white enough, a recent advertising invention. It makes you worry that you secretly reek of body odor and no one wants to tell you, but they all gag behind you in the elevator at work.

The American Dream means you take care of the basics, and don't listen to commercials about what is important.

The American Day Dream tells you that all that matters is getting into a good college. It tells you that your life will be made or broken based on the college you attend. It tells you that any amount of debt is worth it for this class membership. They are wrong. The American Day Dream tells you to get into horrible debt, and it's OK because you will get a fantastic job and be able to pay it all back. Not true.

The American Dream tells of a young person who works hard and is honest and can support themselves and their family.

You need to start identifying the American Day Dream and its influence all around you.

Debt has always been a very un-American thing. It's only for the last sixty or so years that debt has been sold as OK - and it took a lot of advertising to get there.

Americans have needed debt to maintain their standard of living for a while. Americans were, for most of this country's existence, repelled by debt. There was a very strong prejudice against it.

We need to get back to the American Dream in this country. And nothing is more fundamentally American than starting your own career.

Where To Start

First Question: Do you want to be a software developer?

A lot of people think only of the money when they answer this question. There are certain realities about programming software:

- Can you be happy sitting in the same seat all day long, working at your computer?
- Are you willing to continue reading about software after work hours?

- Can you work through the inevitable bugs that will always appear in your program?
- Will you NOT get angry with the software testers when they find something to fix in your program?
- Are you willing to change yourself to do this work?
- Will you spend four hours a day, seven days a week, for six months, learning and practicing software development? Be prepared for that level of work.

You can spend years procrastinating about which language to start with, so I will help you. Start with Python. That's it. Stop thinking about it and get to work.

Right now you are learning how to program. You will be using Python to learn to program. It is only your starting point.

Ta da! Problem solved.

For high school kids

Raspberry Pi!

There is a great little computer called Raspberry Pi. It sells for $35 to $65 on Amazon and other places. Raspberry Pi is a bare-bones computer that will fit in your pocket. You can buy a plastic case to make it easier to carry around.

More importantly, a Raspberry Pi can be connected to an old computer monitor, keyboard, and mouse that someone else has thrown away. For very little money, you can build your own computer. This would be a fun and cheap way for a kid to teach themselves to program in Python.

In fact, there is an entire non-profit that will show you how to learn to program using the Raspberry Pi. See raspberrypi.org and myraspberry-pi.org. Many of these projects are very beginner level, but there are resources all over the web to advance your skills for free.

Must-Haves

There are some basic skills you need to have before you start anything.

1. Touch type. This is a must. All software developers touch type. If you peck at a keyboard with two fingers, then get a basic typing book and teach yourself touch typing. You don't have to be great at it, but you should be able to do at least thirty words a minute. Consider it a way to exercise your discipline and willingness to become a software developer.

2. Know how to write, i.e. spelling and grammar. No one wants to hand a project over to an employee and have the result of their work read like a text message from their dog. Know about full sentences, subjects, predicates, clauses, and punctuation. Fundamentally, that knowledge is what separates someone

who is going to get promoted from someone who isn't. Because I promise you, everyone at the top of an organization knows what a properly written letter or email looks like. If someone has to ask you what you were saying, or to reword what you have written so that they can understand it, you have failed.

3. Manage Yourself. This means show up on time, whether or not the boss is in the office that day. Ask for a deadline for every project and always meet it. Be able to absorb feedback and use it to improve your work. Don't gossip or spread rumors at work. This is the same as "don't shit where you eat." These are qualities every employer is looking for.

4. Oh, and you have to know math. If you aren't good at math, see below.

Learn Software Development for Free

The Python Programming Language has a lot of information at python.org. Click on the Beginners Guide link on the front page to reach a list of downloads and text editors and code samples for you to look at. This is where the real work starts. Go through every exercise.

Another place to learn is looking at bithub.com. It is free and more advanced. Ask questions. Never be afraid to ask questions.

If you want a more structured learning environment, consider taking a class at coursera.org/learn/python.

Another option is udacity.com/course/programming-foundations-with-python--ud036.

codecademy.com/learn/python provides a basic course, with follow-up lessons as your skills advance.

Try to write a program to calculate how many seconds you have been alive. Then write another program to do that in another way. Repeat.

Then write a program that can handle a start date in ancient Greece. And when the pyramids were built. And Stonehenge. And the Big Bang.

Read these websites and blogs:

- Stuff you need to Code Better! - codebetter.com
- Coding Style Guides for Mozilla, Google Java, C++
- CS 106B: Programming Abstractions - cs106b.stanford.edu
- How do I debug my program? - ericlippert.com
- Ten Principles for Good Design by Dieter Rams - archdaily.com
- How to become a programmer, or the art of Googling well - okepi.wordpress.com
- Programming Isn't Manual Labor, But It Still Sucks - mashable.com
- Things I Wish Someone Had Told Me When I Was Learning How to Code - medium.freecodecamp.com
- What are some bad coding habits you would recommend a beginner avoid getting into?

- Lessons from a lifetime of being a coder - thecodist.com
- Hackr.io - Find & share the best online programming courses & tutorials.

Beyond the Basics

Remember, you are learning how to code, not making a decision for the rest of your life. Stop stalling and do it. You are learning how to code with Python for now. Later, this book will show you how to decide where to focus your learning efforts to get a job.

Continue with the previously-mentioned online classes and exercises.

FantasticOranges on Reddit advises ambitious Python programmers to automate the boring stuff with python, and use the latest stable version of python 3. "Don't learn python the hard way." "Anyone that refuses to include Py3 content on a Python learning environment... should be ignored." From Observantguy on Reddit.

MyCodeSchool on YouTube has great lessons on general and specific programming topics. Subscribe.

Read these websites and blogs:

CodesDope
CS 97SI: Introduction to Programming Contests

USER INTERFACE DESIGN: free tech design programs
focusing on human computer interaction.

The Next Step

"Programming is not a spectator sport." So, practice often. Learn algorithms and data structures so that you're not re-inventing the wheel without knowing about it. Read other people's code. - From Reddit user yoshers16.

Professional developers work on programs with millions of lines of code. They are assigned a piece and given a problem to solve. It is a much different process than writing a simple program. That is why just knowing a programming language is not enough.

Software Frameworks

From Wikipedia: A Web framework is a collection of packages or modules which allow developers to write Web applications or services without having to handle such low-level details as protocols, sockets or process/thread management.

Learn about software frameworks, which are a group of software applications that are used in conjunction with each other. For Python, one software framework is Pygame.

Learn about Pygame from coursera.org and Python Programming Tutorials. Refer to wiki.python.org/moin.webframeworks.

Do it. Now.

Learn Data Structures and Algorithms

Geeksforgeeks.org has problems for you to practice.

MyCodeSchool on YouTube has videos to watch.

As a reference book, Introduction to Algorithms by Cormen, Leiserson, Rivest, and Stein, otherwise known as CLRS is well-known. Another handy book is The Algorithm Design Manual by Steven S. Skiena.

See also: https://hackr.io/tutorials/learn-data-structures-

algorithms Look at Wikipedia:
- List of algorithms
- List of algorithm general topics
- List of software development philosophies.

Size Matters

Your computer program may be great for searching a list of cities and states in the U.S., or even the world. But what about a list of information a thousand times bigger than that? How you approach sorting the data within your program will make a big difference in the performance of your application. So know this stuff. Frequently the algorithm you use to manipulate the data will change depending on the size of the data set. The purpose of that choice is to improve the speed of the search. Know about that, too.

Prototype

Talented programmers take one month to write a version of the program that is slow and buggy, like a clay car, and the throw it away and do it in another language. It is not about the programming language. It's about the problem you solve.

But I Can't Do Math!

From dfbkt on Reddit:

"Give web development a try. There are a lot of facets to it, and it can involve as little or as much math as you want it to. You can do anything from a simple static page to a full blown complex web application that does tons of math. I think it's a good thing for practical money making, whether you want to find a job doing it full time or do it in the evenings on the side.

'There are a lot of frameworks out there for web development, but I'd suggest just doing things locally and simply on your own PC to start. Just create a file in notepad and make a simple html page, learn how to add inline JavaScript to it and make the buttons change color or something when you click them. Once you're comfortable there, then try moving that inline script code out into its own file and then try out something like jQuery.

'Just keep building bit by bit, if you like books try that after you learn a little about what you want to do. There's a lot of blogs, YouTube content, and more importantly interactive training that sort of gets you running in a sandbox that you didn't have to spend days learning to setup or spend money using a pre-configured VPS from somewhere like Digital Ocean.

'There's a lot of development work to be done in the world that doesn't require any advanced math knowledge. I do custom WordPress sites in the evenings on the side; they pay more than my 9-5 where I develop internal web applications to support the business (invoicing, commission system, etc.) A lot of people hate on WP, and I get it because there's a lot of "crap" there thrown together by people who don't know what they're doing, but it's not a bad deal to come into when you're already experienced building things from scratch or even on a framework."   Couldn't say it better myself.

Know the Software Industry

Read websites for the field you want to be in. They will tell you who just got bought, who just got a big new contract, and any offices opening up in your area.

Make a note of the names you read online and then find their email address. Look at blogs, too.

Every industry has their own words. Learn them. The purpose of those words is to mark who is on the inside, and who is not.

Refer to:

Reddit

- coding • /r/coding
- Computer Science: Theory and Application • /r/compsci
- CS Career Questions • /r/cscareerquestions
- For learning, refreshing, or just for fun! • /r/dailyprogrammer
- programming • /r/programming
- Reverse Engineering • /r/reverseengineering.

Resources

- Programming, Motherfucker
- Dynamics of Software Development by Jim McCarthy, Microsoft
- Bit Twiddling Hacks
- List of Problems - Techie Delight
- Rosetta Code
- DreamInCode.net
- Geeklist
- Programmers Stack Exchange
- Stack Overflow
- XDA-Developers Android Forums
- Bithub
- ACM TechNews
- Ars Technica
- Hacker News
- Lobsters
- TechCrunch
- The Next Web

- VentureBeat
- The Verge.

Getting a Job: Plan of Attack

Software developers are hired because the boss thinks they will:

- Work extra hours to keep up with new technology.
- Deal with difficult people (users, bosses, co-workers) without getting into an argument.
- Sit still for long periods of time (like 8 hours).
- Learn how to debug, test, peer review, take criticism, and be told you made a mistake.
- Be thick-skinned when your bug causes a major failure.
- Sometimes work unsocial hours rushing to meet an impossible deadline.
- Sometimes work unsocial hours maintaining a system with a critical bug.

Sometimes:
- You work for a boss that gives you too much work to do in too little time.
- You are given a task, which you just don't understand.
- You are given a task with way too much time, and you are not assigned another task until the schedule says so, even though you now have nothing to do.
- You will bust a gut getting a system ready for a deadline only to find the whole system has been scrapped before it even goes live.

Deal with it.

Where do you live?

Most computer programmers do not work in Silicon Valley.

You work where you live. Who hires computer programmers where you live? Another way of asking that question is, who are the largest employers in your area? That is who hires computer programmers where you live.

Go to their websites and look up the IT section. What do people and businesses want there? That's what you need to know to get a job at that business. The job market, and demand, differs from place to place.

For example, let's say you live near Duluth, MN. An online search shows that the major industries there are heavy and light manufacturing plants, academics, woolen mills, and health care.

What Do You Learn?

Now that you have narrowed down the list of industries in your area, find out the software development frameworks they use on Wikipedia. In Duluth, a major employer is the University of Minnesota Duluth. Searching their website shows there is an opening for a Technical Analyst. The software listed in that job announcement is SQL and PeopleSoft. So now you know what software they use.

Another major employer in Duluth is UnitedHealthCare. Enter "software" and "information technology" into the job search tool.

The job description lists "Duties that are performed utilizing UNIX/LINUX /Wintel OS, UNIX/LINUX Scripting, Oracle/SQL, Teradata, PERL, Datastage Parallel Extender, Java, Tomcat server, Toad, SAS, MS SSIS/SSRS, Microstrategy and Serena workflow technologies."

Sirrus Aircraft is also a major employer in Duluth. Their industry is manufacturing. A search of open job positions does not include any in the software development field. So go to quora.com and search "aerospace software framework." Review the results and find your answer.

DO NOT USE GOOGLE FOR THIS SEARCH. A Google search will result in a massive list of advertisements for software companies telling you that their product is the industry standard.

You want to know the tools in a software framework for the industries in your area.

A note on job requirements: these are not a literal requirements. You can have most of them, or even some of them, and still apply for the job. The same goes for a degree requirement. You can substitute relevant work experience for that.

If you live in an area that doesn't hire software developers, move!

Research the Target Company

Now you have a target company. Follow the company on LinkedIn. You are not going to find the CEO on LinkedIn, but you will be able to follow the activities of the company.

Find employees of the target company on LinkedIn, and try to link to them. This is not the time to be shy. You never know who will click "Yes" on a whim.

Another avenue of investigation is the company website. Read every press release. Look at the biographies of every person on the site. Where did they go to school? Is there anything in their background that dovetails with yours such that you can one day mention it in a conversation with them? It's funny how a little comment can open doors for you and prompt an otherwise uninterested manager into taking another look at your resume or referring you to a job in another company.

Don't forget the almighty Google, but especially Google Scholar. Google Scholar has an option where you can look up court cases anywhere in the United States. That means court decisions for and against the target business you wish to employ you is available.

Use www.google.com/scholar to see if the company has been involved in any lawsuits. Getting an idea of the problems the company has had in the past is a good way towards understanding how you can convince them of your value. But don't mention the lawsuit.

DON'T: So I saw you were sued because a supplier said you got their order wrong and it cost them a lot of money.

DO: I have experience in troubleshooting inventory systems.

DON'T: That sexual harassment case really hit you guys hard, huh? Don't worry; I have good eyeball control. Bitches are crazy.

DO: Professionalism is an important skill to develop, and one I pride myself on.

DON'T: I have little spikes on my shoes for the ice, so no slip-and-fall injuries here. You know, like when you guys were sued last year?

DO: Preparation is my strong suit.

This information is background only, for use in your head to help you craft answers to questions and pose a few of your own. No one likes to have it pointed out that they messed up, so don't do it. Just mention your assets and let them draw the conclusion that you would be perfect for the company.

Talk to People Face-to-Face

Go to a professional association for your business area. Go to their website. Look up other members. For a newbie software developer, join IEEE and sign up for the computer section. Then go to their meetings and read their newsletters.

Every job is a sales job. You are selling the business' product or service in one way or another, or you are supporting the ones who do. It really helps to see how the entire process works, not just your piece of it. It makes you a better employee, and it provides a foundation for insightful questions during an interview. Managers are relieved to have a self-starter employee.

If you are nervous, remember to focus on the other person and what makes them interesting. The conversation is not about you. It is about them. People love to talk about themselves. So let them. Read the first edition of Making Friends and Influencing People. Only the first edition, the others are crap.

NETWORKING QUESTIONS for SOFTWARE DEVELOPERS:

How did you get started coding?
What websites should I read regularly?
What was your first job?
What's a really useful skill at your company?
Can I take you out to lunch to talk some more about your work?

Networking Basics

Take software developers you meet to lunch. Ask them questions. Very important here is table manners. You will be judged by your table manners. One of the signs of being a professional, i.e., middle class, is that you know the basics about chewing with your mouth closed, using a salad fork and putting your napkin on your lap.

Take your lead from the person you want information from. Your guest will wait for you to order and then will choose something less expensive. Learn this stuff. When hiring someone, the manager also considers whether or not you will "fit in." Manners are a big part of this decision. The rule is to take your cue from the person you are with. If they say "please" and "thank you," also do it. If they put their napkin on their lap, do that. People feel unconsciously comfortable with individuals who mirror their manners back at them. Do not interrupt, laugh too loud or talk too loud. Match the volume of the person you are with. When shaking hands, don't grip harder than the other person. And of course, don't curse.

Networking is a person-to-person thing. Social media may open the door, but real human contact gets them to remember you.

Get a Job

The Person Who Hires You

All people have stupid stories they tell themselves, and people who make hiring decisions are the same. They say to themselves, "Well this guy hasn't worked in two years, so he'll have a hard time getting up in the morning because what he's been doing is lying on his couch for the last two years."

Of course, you know that you have been selling your living room furniture, learning how to score day-old food from grocery stores, shopping at goodwill, and hand knitting presents for your niece and nephew from old unraveled sweaters. You know that it takes a lot of work to eat and keep the lights on when you're broke.

The same is true about a college degree. People will tell themselves: well, my cousin's daughter had to go to college for this, so the guy in front of me needs to do that, too.

We aren't out to change people's thinking. We are going to work with it to get what we want.

Put Yourself in Their Shoes

If you were a middle-aged manager interviewing a young person, what would you want in an employee? Would you want someone who appears to drink a lot and sometimes doesn't remember everything that happened during that time? BTW- if you don't remember what happens when you drink sometimes, you need my other book: Alcoholic or Problem Drinker?

You have to put yourself in the manager's chair when trying to get them to hire you. All day long, middle managers deal with two groups of people: upper management and employees.

Employees get assigned work, and they do it with varying degrees of success. Some employees need to be reminded all the time to get their task done. Some employees will get the task done very quickly but always with sloppy mistakes. Some employees will ignore what you ask them to do and hand in what they think should be done.

And this is only one part of dealing with employees. The other is babysitting. What would your day be like if you had to spend an hour talking to a 45-year-old man about why it really shouldn't matter that his desk is two inches smaller than someone else's? Or if a group of employees decides they don't like someone else in the office and come to you one by one to complain about that person, after having coordinated their stories? Or two people who have a multi-day fight over where the printer is placed? These are only three examples of the kind of petty nonsense that middle managers have to deal with. Don't be one of those people.

Upper management gives deadlines to middle managers that are based on selling products, not on how long it takes to do the work. Basically, the sometimes-crazy thing you are asked to do may not be coming from your boss. So have sympathy for the person.

Resume

Your spelling and grammar must be perfect. Yes, English class mattered. It is the one subject that signals you have a good education. When people see your resume and cover letter, they are looking for grammar and spelling errors. If they don't see any, you are given credit for having intelligence. You may be seeking a job as an engineer and believe that it doesn't matter how good your spelling is. You would be wrong. Bad spelling shows sloppiness, and bad grammar shows ignorance. No one wants to hire that.

Your resume doesn't say who you are. It says, "I can get this job done for you!" It says, "Hire me!" It says, "I am not a problem!" and "I can do the boring parts of computer programming without complaining."

No one is hiring the real you. They are renting what you can do for them. Employers put out a call for people based on what they think they need. Your resume needs to reflect what they think they want, right back at them. See below, The Robot That Hires You.

Don't choose unusual paper or formatting. It says to a prospective employer that you can't work within a system and that you want to be the center of attention. This may be good for an artistic or creative job, as an interior designer, for instance. But not for a software developer.

Create a LinkedIn profile. Link it to code you have written and posted on GitHub and make sure it compiles. Connect to professional organizations through your profile. LinkedIn is also your resume. Fill it in and add links to your code. A college degree or the GPA are only there to show you are not stupid. There are other less expensive ways to do that.

Your resume should show what specific tasks you can complete, not just the name of the software, such as memory management, a random number generator, print queue, database development or design.

Walking Through the Door

"Skills can be taught, professionalism cannot." -

Reddit What Nobody Wants

- Someone who can't get along with other people.
- Someone who steals.
- Someone who might come into the workplace one day and start shooting people.
- Someone with a drug or alcohol problem.

It used to be that you just had to keep controversial stuff off your resume. Now a potential employer can read all about you on social media. Be low risk. You may be young enough to think that showing people that you got drunk is funny, but nobody wants to hire that. So don't post a photo or video of yourself drunk, getting drunk, or committing a crime on the Internet. Anywhere. People want an employee that is no trouble, so look like you are no trouble from their perspective.

Blogs to read about interview preparation:
- Techie Delight.
- CareerCup.
- CSE Blog - quant, math, computer science puzzles.
- Guide to Tech Interviews.
- Here's How to Prepare for Tech Interviews.
- How to Ace an Algorithms Interview.
- LeetCode Online Judge
- Runhe Tian Coding Practice
- Tech Interview.

Understanding Social Media

Use social media to your advantage by adding connections to IEEE and other professional associations related to your goal.

Avoid any speech that implies you may not be able to work with all kinds of people. The thing about working is that you are going to be exposed to people you are not choosing to associate with. You are kind of stuck with them. No manager wants to hire someone who requires special measures because they can't work with, or for a certain group of people.

This is America. There are all kinds of people here. They aren't going anywhere, no matter what you think. They all have some money that your company wants to make theirs. That won't happen if one of their employees is seen as someone who can't get along with albino Pygmies.

Now there may not be a lot of albino Pygmies out there. Your prospective employer may not have great concerns about the albino Pygmy market. But they will be concerned about hiring someone who can't get along with an entire group of people. And not only that, someone who announces it to the world.

So don't do it. The only real race that counts in America is the green dollar.

For example, President Obama smokes cigarettes. So did Jackie Kennedy Onassis. To cultivate a certain image of themselves, neither has had a photo taken of them smoking a cigarette. We all know about these two people, and have opinions about them. But it is in no way based on the visual impression of them smoking, which would alter perceptions of them a great deal.

Now smoking is not illegal. It is not associated with cruelty or animal abuse. But the very picture of someone smoking will alter perceptions about him or her. My point is, you create lasting impressions about yourself by revealing personal information. It could prevent you from getting a job, even if you ace the interview. Don't do that to yourself.

If hiring managers are afraid they might hire an irresponsible person, they will be looking for warning signs in a social media profile of debauchery and useless, hung over employees who call in sick all the time. Of course, they may secretly wish they could do all that, and decide you must be that way, too.

The people hiring you are older. One universal thing about older people: they don't remember all the drugs and drinking they did when they were your age. They also don't remember the laws they broke or all the lies they told to get laid.

That's why you have to clean up your social media profile.

Who They Want to Hire

Potential employers are judging you, and asking themselves the following questions:

- Can you show up on time?
- Can you write an email that others can understand, or is it written in text-speak?
- Are you going to be on your best behavior at a meeting with a client? That means no cursing or slang. Can you sit up straight in a chair, say please and thank you, sit still, and listen unless someone asks you a direct question? You will understand your role is to support the senior person from your team, and you won't complain about the dress code or the food in the cafeteria. As an aside, you will also realize no one cares what you think, but only what you can do for them at work.
- Will you dress and groom yourself like an adult or a child?Specifically, will you need to be told that shorts, flip-flops, belly shirts, spandex, and yoga pants are not appropriate at work?
- Can you park in a parking garage, get parking validated and make it to the correct floor to the correct meeting room on time?
- Can you talk to a senior level employee without slang or cursing?

- Can you admit you don't know something?
- Disciplined enough to come in the earliest?
- Do you want it enough to be the last to leave the office?

What You Need To Have

A well-rounded LinkedIn profile.
Samples of code you have written.
Completed software application that compiles.

A software program that has been fully completed tells several things about you. It says that you have the maturity to start and finish a project, and do not quit when the fun part is over. A completed software program has been tested not just by you, but also by someone else trying to use it. That means, without fail, that your user will find things for you to fix. So fix them.

Another thing a completed software program shows about you is that you have the tenacity and the self-drive to finish a project. That means you won't be the employee who has to be constantly reminded to get things done when the fun part of the job is over.

You won't believe how many software developers hand in their work and then the application won't compile. That means it won't run. If the people hiring you think you aren't the kind of worker who will be doing that, it puts you ahead in the hiring game.

When you work professionally as a software developer, you will be part of a development team. You will be working with other developers on code that has been written already. It is critical that anyone trying to edit code should be able to understand the flow of the computer program. That same obligation applies to your work. That can be seen in how you use whitespace. When a potential employer looks at your work, they want to see that it is formatted in such a way that making changes to it will be easily understandable.

ACTION PLAN

Review the job description.

When reading the job description, determine whether the job is entry level, mid-level, or senior. Then decide on applying. There is no sense on wasting your time and energy trying to land a job that just isn't right for you. Another reason is to apply for jobs with insane qualification requirements that you might otherwise skip.

Find the keywords.

Next, find the keywords for the job description. For this step, look at the required skill list. Which terms are unique to this field? Of course, include those in your resume if you can in any way. But there will also be keywords that are unique to that industry. For example, you may be seeking a software development job at a hospital. There will be keywords for software development and keywords for the health industry. Use both.

Tie your experience to those keywords.

It is not enough to add certain magic words. They need to be tied, somehow, to your experience or training. If you have done something similar, mention that the product you used was similar to the keyworded product. Add as many keywords from that to your resume as possible.

After the dumb computer looks at your resume, the ill-informed HR person looks at it. They don't know that Biology and Zoology are the same degree. They don't think that they have to know that. These are the second gatekeepers in your job search. Remember that and try to communicate your experiences at their level.

The people who read your submitted resume do not know anything about the subject area. Write your qualifications for a well-read generalist who will not understand that Microsoft Word is a part of Microsoft Office and then toss your resume for lack of qualification.

It is best to tailor your resume to the exact job description or have several variations of the same resume that state your qualifications in different ways.

Use https://www.jobscan.co to have your resume analyzed for keywords. Of course, you will have to figure out the keywords by reading. There is a lot of specialization in any field. Specialize your keywords, too. If you want to develop smartphone applications, use those terms. If you want to edit the code for large databases, use those terms.

Try to include what skills you took from a previous job on your resume, rather than just a list of what the job entailed. It shows that you can learn and grow. Don't just list your responsibilities.

Special skills or other accomplishments, like winning a Bronze medal at the Olympics, or holding a Guinness world record, sets you apart from the hundreds of resumes, like being an Eagle Scout. This part is for when a human actually looks at your resume. It will happen eventually.

The cover letter should give an overview of your skills that list the items in the job ad. Include words and phrases from the company mission statement in your cover letter. It shows you did the footwork and know about the company. Include a paragraph about why you want the job.

If you meet 70% of the job description, apply. "Years of experience" = skill level. List related skills with specific examples.

If you don't get the job, follow it up with a polite thank you and a request of what you may have done better. Make as many contacts and friends in HR positions as possible, this is a great resource and is very often neglected

Make their job easier. Attach a letter of reference to your resume so that no one has to make phone calls if they choose you for an interview.

7% Will Be Fired in Two Years

You are not finished when you get the job. That point is only the beginning.

Many employers hire new employees with the idea that 7% of them will be fired in two years. It's called "attrition." So as soon as you start your job, you are competing against your co-hires to still be there in 2 years.

Keep that mindset in deciding to get to work early, don't waste time at work, and delivering your work on time.

Getting the Next Job

You will get future jobs by being recommended by your co-workers. Recruiters are very expensive; no one wants to use one. Also, recruiters have the attention spans of crack addicts. They get together on Mondays and compare notes on jobs that need to be filled, and it's as if the previous 52 weeks never happened. Just expect it. And they are very expensive; any company saves a lot of money by getting references from someone they are hiring instead of using headhunters. Keep that in mind regarding how you treat your coworkers.

They will be your source of jobs for the rest of your career.

Conclusion

If you are willing to work hard, study on your own and work on your own time to learn new skills, you can be a software developer.

The actions in this book provide a roadmap to becoming a software developer without going to college. It is a series of steps that other software development professionals I interview took to get there, and you can too.

The most important thing, and the hardest, will be to stick to the roadmap after a few weeks, when the initial excitement wears off. I am sitting here on a beautiful afternoon, typing on my computer with no idea if anyone will read this book. My Mom will buy a copy, but probably won't read it. Many days in the past year have been spent working without any guarantee of result. I just have to do the work anyway.

I may not know if this book will sell more than ten copies, but if I don't write it, I know it won't. So take the risk. There is a need for software developers, and you can meet that need if you work at it.

Let me know how it works out.

About the Author

Christine Axsmith grew up in a area where most people didn't go to college. Later, her career took a sharp left turn after taking a stand against waterboarding at the CIA. See her entry in <u>Wikipedia.org</u>. From there, she reinvented herself as the owner of a successful dog walking company, a guardian for the elderly and disabled, a trial attorney and a writer. These experiences taught her how to learn from successful people and to draw a roadmap to recreate their success. In recent years, as lawyers started getting replaced by software, it sparked Christine Axsmith's interest in this topic.

Christine Axsmith has been published by NIST and NSA regarding information security law, has presented papers at MIT conferences and the International Bar Association, and actively participated in the United Nations Commission on International Trade Law - Electronic Commerce Working Group. Her research on encryption export became required reading at Harvard Law School.

She uses her extensive research skills to provide a roadmap for non-college success in her books by interviewing self-made millionaires and other people in the many fields.

There are many media reports about success without college statistics, and many of them will tell you that the income a person earns is dramatically increased with a college degree. That was the old days. More than that, only a little over half of college students get a four year degree. Now, when calculating whether college is a good "investment," you need to include the cost of student loans.

Other books by this author

Please visit your favorite ebook retailer to discover other books by Christine Axsmith:

$uccess Without College Roadmap Series
Roadmap to Software Developer
Roadmap to Plumber
Frankenstein - The Robot That Hires You

Connect with Christine Axsmith

I really appreciate you reading my book! Here are my social media coordinates:

$uccess Without College - Roadmapto Software Developer
www.successwithoutcollege.net
podcast:Success Without College
Instagram:SuccessWithoutCollege
Twitter:@SuccessWithout2

www.ingramcontent.com/pod-product-compliance
Lightning Source LLC
Chambersburg PA
CBHW051215050326
40689CB00008B/1324